INTO THE
WOLF

Poems by Robert Best

First published 2023 by IRON Press
5 Marden Terrace
Cullercoats
North Shields
NE30 4PD
tel +44(0)191 2531901
ironpress@xlnmail.com
www.ironpress.co.uk
Find us on Facebook

ISBN 978-1-8383444-5-0
Printed by Imprint Digital

Text © Robert Best 2023

Cover and book design, Brian Grogan and Peter Mortimer
Typeset in Georgia 10pt

IRON Press books are distributed by IPS UK
and represented by Inpress Ltd
Milburn House, Dean Street
Newcastle upon Tyne NE1 1LF
tel: +44(0)191 2308104
www.inpressbooks.co.uk

List of Poems

Frozen Moments	5
Copper Cable & Hungry Ghosts	6
Nine Millimetre	8
She Always Wears Purple	9
Fine Rain	10
Falling More Slowly	11
Into the Wolf	12
Peace in Death	13
Flaming Sambuca	15
Let Him Dance	17
The Shamanic Poet	18
Mischievous Herald	19
Three Occasions When Dad Saved My Life	20
A Symphony of Pain	25
No Separation	28
The Exhibition	29
Steel in the Breeze	30
When Quarks Go Queer	31
Acquainted With The Divine	32
A Perfect Start to Autumn	33
Every Moment, in This Moment	34

Foreword

YOU'RE HERE LOOKING FOR AN ORIGIN STORY, RIGHT?
WELL, YOU'RE IN LUCK! I HAVE SEVERAL TO CHOOSE FROM...

Do you want to hear the one about the little boy who loved writing poetry at school, and who even won a prize for a two-stanza piece about the moon? He made a little pamphlet of his poetry, aged about seven; just a few pages, bound up with string, that sits on my bookshelf to this day.

Or how about, 'It was 2017 when I realised, properly and deeply and for the very first time, at an event in the back of a small pub in Newcastle, that poetry is, at its core, a spoken word art form'?

I regularly have great ideas, and, for many years, I would take one and dive straight into planning an article, an essay, or a short story, always with great excitement. I would usually begin with a research phase and, after a few hours (including many tangents and dead ends) I'd suddenly find that all the magic had drained away from the original idea, and the empty, dry husk that remained no longer interested me. Now, following that inspiring epiphany in Newcastle, I'll take an idea and run with it into poetry, into verse, and often, the magic just flows and grows.

I'm inspired by whatever interests me in the moment, and I'm interested in pretty much everything. Above all, though, I have a deep love and connection to the wild places, the remote places, the places where the hares rarely lay eyes on people; where the streams are clean enough to drink; where the silence can be overwhelming; and where I can be physically and spiritually close to the beings, the seen and the unseen, who inhabit those realms. This connection is greatly illuminated by the shamanic and esoteric practices and world view I have developed over many decades, in which Spirit is constantly communicating with me – with all of us. I choose to pay attention, in the moment, and allow the wisdom and the insights to flow.

My world view serves me well. And sometimes, it serves up poetry.

Frozen Moments

I am a balloon,
Filled up with whiskey –
Single malt –
Suspended over a candle flame.

I am a clapperboard house,
Paint peeling, windows nailed shut,
In the path of a tornado.

I am a Ming dynasty vase,
Imperious, nonchalant,
And in the way
Of a hammer hurled.

I am a golf club,
Five iron, head gleaming,
Swung high, calling down
The lightning bolt.

Copper Cable & Hungry Ghosts

Hong Kong, 1990.
The Bank of China Tower opens and,
Buried deep in the bowels of the basement
The computer systems refuse to work.
Panic sets in.
The feng shui consultant is called back
And he rapidly realises that which is remiss.
He had recommended that a ring of copper cable
Should encircle the basement
And the builders had ignored him.
Or forgotten.
Quickly, the copper ring is installed.
Immediately, the computer systems hum into life
And have barely missed a beat, or a byte, since.

Newry, 1982.
A hard, Republican town
Full of hard, Republican men,
Where a council worker refused
To cut down a hawthorn tree
Because it was known as the heart of a faerie ring.
In desperation,
When none of his colleagues would wield the axe,
The council offered a reward
Of two hundred and fifty pounds
To anyone willing to cut down the tree.
Poverty was rife, yet no one stepped forward,
And the hawthorn thrives there still.

In Iceland
The elves hold sway.
A crew drilling for water in the North
Experience multiple and unexplained equipment failures
Until they move away from the cliffs
Known to be home to the 'huldufolk'.
Then, the drills restart
And water is found.
Roads get diverted around important elven-rocks,
Or the rocks themselves are carefully relocated,
Thirty tons or more,
At great expense.

Every night, back in Hong Kong,
After the Mass Transit Railway has closed for the night,
They run a single, empty train, once, around the whole network,
So the hungry ghosts can get back home.

Nine Millimetre

Jericho. Tanfoglio. Heckler & Koch.
Luger, Ruger, Bauer, Lerker, Remington and Glock.
DiamondBack, Ashani.
Springfield and Benelli.
TriStar Chiappa,
Vektor and Zastava.

Browning. Jennings. Century Arms and Kahr.
Taurus, Kel-Tec, Zenith; CZ, Makarov and Steyr.
Magnum, Colt and Uzi,
Stechkin, Astra, Lahti,
Kongsberg and Korovin,
Bersa, Smith & Wesson.

She Always Wears Purple

Ilargi, Kuu and Luna.
Chang Xi, Chia, Diana.
The Moon Goddess has a thousand names
But she always wears purple.

moon shot moon river blue moon Reverend Moon
moon cake dark moon full moon blood moon

Ask for the moon and be over the moon.
Bark at the moon, then become the moon.
Moon around, promise the moon, shoot for the moon
And give thanks, from your heart, to the Man in the Moon
Who loyally serves Phoebe, Artemis, Gleti,
Mano, Mahina, Mayari,
Mama Killa and Jaci and Selardi
Lona and Menily and Hanwi.

The Moon Goddess has a thousand names
But she always wears purple.

Fine Rain

Sometimes,
    Walking Molly, late at night,
    I see, blowing past the old street light,
    Rain so fine it's barely mist
    By which my brow feels barely kissed.

Sometimes,
    Up on the moors in quickening gales
    And Northumbrian rain that never fails
    To drench and soak, runs down my neck,
    Replenishing river, lake and beck.

Some time ago,
    When the Earth was cooling in the void,
    Water arrived by asteroid.
    Every drop's been here a billion years;
    Once, that rain was dinosaur tears.

Falling More Slowly

It was relief she'd felt, stepping off the ledge,
Fourteen floors above the street.
Years living in misery; hours standing on the edge,
And now, choosing to die at strangers' feet.

In her mind, where she'd rehearsed this many times,
She'd seen herself holding a sky-diver position,
Even adjusting slightly to change her lines
To avoid killing some innocent other, in a collision.

Instead, she found herself tumbling, spinning, her long skirt –
The yellow one her sister gave her two birthdays back –
Binding her legs as one, as she prayed this wouldn't hurt,
At least, not for long. Not after the first crack.

Then a sudden up-rush of warm air stopped her dizzy spin;
Arms open, skirt now billowing, she felt almost holy.
As the thermal took her anger, her sadness, her sin,
She realised, with a smile, she was falling more slowly.

Into the Wolf

I was in the second half of my first half-marathon
When I first saw the wolf.
Thick grey pelt and huge splayed paws,
Patting the snow as it padded through the forest –
Lub-dub, lub-dub, lub-dub.
It can keep this up for hours.

I was in the third fifth of my first half-marathon
When my viewpoint suddenly changed.
Where before I was hovering just above, just behind,
And just off the wolf's left side,
Now I sit astride his powerful neck,
Feel his shoulders rippling beneath me,
Our mingled breath a procession of wispy phantoms
Left behind in the biting Arctic air.

Lub-dub, lub-dub, lub-dub, lub-dub.

In the final sixth of my first half-marathon,
I finally shifted into the wolf.
Synching with his rhythm, lub-dub, lub-dub,
Breathing his breath, lub-dub, lub-dub,
Seeing at his level, seeing through his eyes
Ultra-violet trees and multi-spectrumed snow,
Keeping this up for hours, lub-dub, lub-dub.

I ran my first half-marathon in a reasonable time,
Yet remembering the moment when I crossed the line
I wonder – how much of me was human in that moment?
And how much of me was lupine?

Peace in Death

I was struck by the phrase
In an article on Afghanistan;
'Peace in death', said the man.
I was struck by the phrase.

In an article on Afghanistan,
Boys blow themselves up in crowded places,
Parting limbs from torsos, heads from faces,
In an article on Afghanistan,

Boys blow themselves up in crowded places.
Yet I saw peace in death when my sister died
With my parents and I right by her side;
Boys blow themselves up in crowded places.

Yet I saw peace in death when my sister died,
Death wiping her face clear of pain,
Of stress, of lines, of fear, every stain;
Yet I saw peace in death when my sister died,

Death wiping her face clear of pain.
Is peace in death a lament or a longing,
For solitary silence or a sense of belonging?
Death wiping her face clear of pain;

Is peace in death a lament or a longing?
I was struck by the phrase
Virgins in Paradise, Praise!
Is peace in death a lament or a longing?

I was struck by the phrase
In an article on Afghanistan;
'Peace in death', said the man.
I was struck by the phrase.

Flaming Sambuca

The glass is small, thick, heavy,
Shaped like an elongated bell
Emerging from a squashed-ball base.

The alcohol pours like clear satin,
Calmly making the space its own,
The meniscus curving like a sly smile.

Coffee beans are dropped in and float
Incongruously, like tiny dark dug-outs.
Three for the purists; four is just showing off.

It takes skill to conjure flames from liquid –
Are we lighting the drink here, or the fumes above?
They're electric blue at first, and almost invisible.

Tiny wrinkles press up to the inside of the glass
Like fingerprints. The beans begin to boil and bubble –
They are the catalyst that changes everything.

The blue flame dons an orange mantle
As each bean releases a brown spike
Of gently sinking melt. As above, so below.

As the flame peaks, and the spikes bottom out,
It's time to blow out the fire and pause,
Patiently, for quick lips do burn and blister!

The scent that arises on the tiny thermal
Is of aniseed and cedar wood, cicadas,
And a Columbian barista undertone.

The first lift to the lips is pure sensory overload.
The first sip heady, warm, spicy,
And it slides down the throat with its sharp claws out.

I like to sip, but not too slowly,
Timing it so there's a little heat left,
Even as the last drop glides past the beans well spent.

Let Him Dance

Have you any idea
How hard it can be
For a man to show his feelings?
To get emotional?
To unblock the flow of tears?
To – heaven forfend! – be vulnerable?

So when your man
Wants to dance,
You let him dance.

The Shamanic Poet

Every word is steeped in mystery.
Every line emerges from the crack
Between the Worlds.
Every stanza bears the blessings of Spirit,
And every verse is layered in meaning.

Come closer, for there is more to tell!

The ink shapeshifts onto the page,
From the confines of cartridge
To carve wisdom onto the bark of the world,
Conjuring memories from the paper
Of the forest, of which once it was a part,
And from which it has never truly left.

The Poet writes from Dream, from Innocence;
Not merely a passive channel,
But as a mischievous herald,
A passionate creator,
A bridge between the Worlds,
Seeking a higher Truth.

The Mischievous Herald

The mischievous Herald
Calls to others to come play
In the higher vibrations
Where Divine Sparks hold sway.
Identities quieten;
The still, small voice speaks out,
And greatness steps forward,
Offers guidance beyond doubt.
The compassion and the wisdom,
The poetry and prose
Shows the Way to the Seeker
And behold! The seeker rose
To the pivot of the pendulum,
Above its vicious swing,
To acknowledge his identity
Yet away from its harsh sting.
The mischievous Herald
Calls others to come play
In the higher vibrations
Where Divine Sparks hold sway.

Three Occasions
When Dad Saved My Life

i. When I was a boy,
   Dad used to take me to watch the scrambling.
   Scrambles are motorcycle races –
   Dirt bikes racing around a muddy field,
   The track marked out with thick, hessian rope
   Strung between wooden stakes
   Hammered into the earth that very morning.
   There was usually a sign somewhere –
   'Motor Sport is Dangerous' –
   But stand where you like
   As long as you're on the spectator side
   Of the timber-and-hessian safety barrier.

   One day,
   We're standing on the outside of a right-hand bend,
   Near a hawthorn tree,
   Dad taking photographs with his Minolta SLR
   Of the bike-and-sidecar combinations
   Careering towards us, then past us,
   Trailing peacock tails of dirt and stones.

   Mid-race,
   Through the blue haze of two-stroke smoke,
   Over the roaring din of engines,
   Through the excitement and testosterone,
   Dad suddenly yelled, 'Let's move!'
   We'd walked no more than five paces up the hill
   When a combination lost control on the bend,
   Crashing through the barrier,

Snapping two fence posts like matchsticks,
Running over the rope
Before running over the very spot where we'd been standing
A few seconds before.

ii. I was a young teenager
When Dad took me to Zante
For a two-week holiday.
There was no airport.
It took 24 hours to get there.
Car.
Train.
London Underground.
Aeroplane from Heathrow to Athens.
Taxi.
Coach to the west coast.
Ferry to the island.
Minibus to our villa.
It was raining when we arrived;
The first time it had rained in August in living memory.

Dad hired a motorcycle for a few days.
Explore the island. Meet the real locals.
I remember walking into a taverna, way up in the hills,
Looking for lunch,
And being greeted by sudden silence, like I'd seen in the
Westerns.
Heading back to the villa on a good road –
Shorts, t-shirts, no helmets –
A little three-wheel truck in front,
Carrying lengths of timber way longer than itself,
Turned off right and briefly disappeared,
Only to start reversing into our path moments later.

It was too late to brake,
Especially on gravel, that acts like ball bearings
To a bike in distress.
Instead, thinking fast, Dad leant the bike down
Hard left, as we leant hard right
And the timber ends passed through the gap we'd just created,
Brushing the hairs on my forearm.

Dad pulled over a mile or so later
And we sat in the pine-scented shade,
Listening to the cicadas
Until his hands stopped shaking.

iii. Breakfast time, Boxing Day, 1989,
And I'm driving myself to the railway station,
Going back to work in London for a few days.
Dad's in the passenger seat
So he can drive my car back home for me.
Only a few miles out
The car twitches. Black ice.
I regain control.
We just have time to remark on it
When it goes again, properly this time;
The back end swings out right,
The front wheels mount the curb,
And we're sliding sideways, fast,
Towards a large and solid road sign.
I see it looming in my side window.
'Oh, Dad', I remember saying.

My next memory is screaming.
Screaming from the searing pain –

Pain my brain has long since blocked out.
The 90-degree bend in the middle of the drivers' door
Has punched a 90-degree bend in the middle of my right femur.
My right foot is still over near the accelerator pedal –
Crazy angles –
And with both legs jammed firmly against the centre consul
And the door immovable
I'm trapped, in intense agony, for thirty-five minutes.
Dad's out, unhurt, but screaming in his own torment
As he believed
In that moment,
As he later told me,
That the car was about to burst into flames
And roast me alive.

Later – weeks later –
After the hospital, the operation, out on crutches,
We visit the wreck at a local garage.
The entire chassis is bent by a foot and a half!
But I'm intrigued by the roof,
Caved in by the same pole, to the same 90 degrees as the door,
Creating a sharp, inward jag of metal
At roughly temple height.
Only then did Dad tell me that,
A second or so before impact,
He'd reached over, arm around my shoulders,
And pulled me down.
I crashed with my head resting safely on his lap.

iv. Ten years later,
    Dad slipped and fell on some hotel steps in Kathmandu.

Eventually, they discovered a crumbling vertebra.
While recovering, the digestive disorders began.
Firm reassurances from the GP
Were eventually followed
By a bowel cancer diagnosis.
'Untreated, you have less than a year', they said.
'With chemo, you've got at least two.'
He went for the chemo and was dead in nine months.

A week or so before he died at home,
In his own bed,
In a memory I can never un-see,
He's standing in the bathroom, supported by my Mum,
With his back to me,
Shaking and skeletal, like those wretches out of Belsen.
The last time I saw him alive
He was unconscious on morphine.
I kissed him on the cheek
And he puckered his lips in response.
I know he knew it was me;
I had a goatee beard at the time
Which he would have felt on his face.

You saved my life three times, Dad.
Yet, when you were dying, I could only stand by and cry.

A Symphony of Pain

How's the pain now? asked the nurse.
Like I'm buried neck-deep in a nest of fire ants.

a never forgotten scene
in a long-forgotten novel;
>
> the victim is staked out
> spread-eagled
> on the desert sand
> and his torturer –
> just as the sun comes up –
> 'surgically removes'
> his eyelids.

How's the pain now? asked the nurse.
It feels like I'm bathing in hydrochloric acid.

> Simon Weston describes
> running through the burning ship
> set alight
> by Argentinian missiles
> and passing a fellow sailor
> who had been thrown
> against a red-hot
> steel bulkhead
> and is stuck to it,
> screaming,
> as his flesh melts
> into the metal.

How's the pain now? asked the nurse.
Like being peeled and rolled in rock salt.

> Idi Amin
> had a prisoner tied down
> face up on a bench.
> A rat would be placed
> on his abdomen,
> kept in place
> by an upturned metal bucket
> strapped to the victim.
> A fire was lit on the bucket.
> As the heat inside
> became unbearable
> for the rat
> it would try to escape
> the only way open to it –
> by gnawing and clawing
> it's way
> down.

How's the pain now? asked the nurse.
Like being dipped in molten glass
Where not all the glass has quite melted
And sharp shards continue to scratch and puncture
Me.

A memory.
Boxing Day, 1989.
A BMW
slides sideways
on black ice
until the centre of the drivers' door
hits an immovable signpost
creating a 90-degree bend in the door
that punches a 90-degree break
in my right femur.
Trapped in the car
for thirty long minutes
I screamed like a siren
but (sadly) I didn't pass out.

No Separation

'Invite God into your heart', the wizard was told.
'It's powerful practice. It's spiritual gold.'
So he did, every night, while falling asleep,
And symbols rushed at him; whales from the deep,
Mustangs on the prairie, hares in mid-leap,
Crosses within circles, a star glinting red,
Waterfalls and rainbows, Tracey Emin's bed.
From symbols flowed insights, but God never came.
Perhaps, thought the wizard, I'm calling the wrong name.

As the symbols slowly dwindled, a new insight dawned –
Obvious and startling, it arrived fully formed –
'If God is in all things, then God is in me!'
'I can't invite Him in to where He must already be!'
Soon this was superseded by a deeper Truth still;
Omniscient God, through the power of His will,
Shattered Himself into countless Divine Sparks
To experience detachment, the lights and the darks,
And the wizard exclaimed, 'One of those Sparks is me!
I AM God! I AM One! Now I finally see!'

No invitation needed. There's no one to invite!
There's no real separation of the person from the Light.

The Exhibition

The Grand Exhibition of 1848
Had the world all a-quiver and agog.
The venue walls shimmered with polished silver plate,
Rising up from an uninspired bog.

Inside there were paintings of Air and of Earth;
A live dandy, dressed in silk, in a cage.
In a curtained-off oasis, humpbacks giving birth
While a shaman chanted songs and smouldered sage.

They'd shipped in a rainforest, complete with the rain,
And a glacier on the backs of five geese.
A mother-of-pearl chamber held sparks of pure pain;
Guests cried, 'Will these wonders never cease?'

But the Fountain of Mercury has long since dried up,
And the sand eels ate away the silver plate.
The dandy escaped, and stole the calf-skull cup,
Leaving the humpbacks, and the shaman, to their fate.

Steel in the Breeze

I walk, through the languid, lurid, lazy air of early summer,
Breathing in the warmth, the scent of light rain on freshly cut grass,
The abundance and fertility humming in the air, softly breathless;
I hear it only as the sound left behind through the bevelled fracture in the silence.

I host a swarm of black flies in the vortex behind my head.
I say a swarm – maybe a dozen or so individuals,
My dirtily droning disciples, little more than an irritation
Until one goes aural, ocular, oral.

Sometimes, a lower note, a slower flight,
Like a Hercules among Spitfires; like a buzzard, mobbed from above by three crows;
Like a heron taking off across a field of swooping swallows.
Slower of wit and reaction, too – easy to swat,
Even to pluck from the air and crush in my fist.
Ah, but the horsefly more than makes up for its languid approach to the world –
A cunning, conniving combination of a breeze-light touch when it lands on bare skin
And a pair of steel mandibles, for a nip that lasts for hours.

When Quarks Go Queer

When a didgeridoo meets a didgeridon't
It's a matter of chance if they will or they won't
Each collapse the other's waveform and then fizzle out,
Disappear down a wormhole, like a quantum waterspout
To reappear in a Universe, parallel to here,
Where a small rip in space-time, a rupture, a tear,
Causes molecules to mix up and quarks to go queer –
Didgeridoo and didgeridon't are no longer, I fear!
Sub-atomic confusion has delivered instead,
A fossilised halibut, and a three-poster bed.

Acquainted With The Divine
(after 'Acquainted With the Night' by Robert Frost)

All things are connected in Time and Space.
I sense this deeply when I lie in bed –
I see the Cosmic fabric interlace.

God's not a bearded man with halo'd head;
God's not part jackal, elephant or dog;
God takes whatever form your teacher said.

Divine's a vibration – cuts through the fog
of holy books that just serve to divide,
trapping the blinded in an ancient bog.

We all arrived here, so we all decide
whether to acknowledge the Spark within,
nurture the Divine Light that shines inside

this suit of bones and organs, flesh and skin.
My Divine's eternal, and without sin.

A Perfect Start to Autumn

The late September morning
When I stepped out and realised
That the last of the swallows
Had left for the winter,
I went back to bed and wept.
Wept for the loss of friends,
For the end of a glorious summer,
For skies no longer cleaved
Into graceful arcs,
For the reminder of time passing
With nothing to show.

Early the following morning
I leapt out of bed
At the cries of geese
And saw fifty or more
Flying low over my cottage
In a perfect vee formation,
In a perfect start to any day.
In a perfect start to autumn.

Every Moment, in This Moment

The light from the sun
Takes 8 minutes and 20 seconds
To reach the Earth.
In this moment, you are seeing the sun as it was
8 minutes and 20 seconds ago.

Alpha Centauri is 4.3 light years away,
So stand today,
Warming your toes on our second nearest star –
It's just a little warmer than the surface of our sun –
And look back on the Earth as it was
4.3 years ago.

Seen from Alpha Centauri
Our love is still alive, and thriving.
4.3 years ago we were walking on the beach in Wales
Where I taught you to skim flat stones
Out across the smooth water
Between the waves.
I massaged your glistening, willing body
In that hot, humid hotel room near Smithfield Market
And when we were spent, and sated,
We went out to the bars without showering,
Trailing pheromones after us, like a veil.

You could stand on Alpha Centauri
And watch us move into our house in the country
With your girls –

The day when the wild horses galloped down from the fells,
The herd parting around our car,
Re-joining beyond, flowing onwards and out of sight.

On a bridge of light stretching
From Earth to Alpha Centauri and beyond,
Every moment is playing out still –
Every moment, in this moment.

ROBERT BEST has been a farm labourer in Northumberland, a stockbroker in the City of London, a university lecturer in South Korea, a project director for a software developer, a strategist, consultant, investor, and author.

Much of his poetic inspiration arises from his decades-long study and practice of shamanism, our oldest belief system. This practice, in turn, grew out of the fifteen years he spent studying with a ritual Kabbalistic group in London.

Robert helped to create a new UK bank, and now works as an academic editor.

He lives in the wilds of Northumberland with his son (sometimes) and three-and-a-half cats.

Publication Credits

Falling More Slowly	PoetCrit (Vol. 34, No. 2) July 2021
Peace in Death	October Hill Magazine (Vol.4, Issue 4) January 2021
The Shamanic Poet	As Above, So Below (Issue 5) May 2020
The Mischievous Herald	PoetCrit (Vol.34, No.2) July 2021
Three Occasions When Dad Saved My Life	October Hill Magazine (Vol.4, Issue 2, converted into a short story on request)
The Exhibition	The Oldie (competition winner) March 2019
A Perfect Start to Autumn	PoetCrit (Vol. 34, No. 2) July 2021

The following were first published by PoetsOnline.org
She Always Wears Purple (May 2019)
Flaming Sambuca (October 2022)
Acquainted With the Divine (October 2018)
Every Moment, in This Moment (August 2018)

Please visit www.shamanicpoet.com for the complete selection of Robert's published works.